Sweeping the Porch

First Edition
ISBN: 978-1-963110-23-4

Published by
Pine Row Press
www.pinerow.com

For permissions or inquiries, please contact:
Pine Row Press
Ft Mitchell, KY
contact@pinerow.com

Sweeping the Porch

poems by

Sharon Perkins Ackerman

Pine Row Press

Ft Mitchell, KY

For my grandmother

Contents

I

II

I

Behold, I tell you a mystery: We shall not all sleep,
but we shall all be changed—

—1 Corinthians 15:51

A Dry Spell in July They Say is Climate Change

Not much to notice in the meadow—
mostly daisies panhandling
for rain. Blackberries run right up
to you though, stretch their arms,
praising the Lord from a dusty row.
It's hard not to admire things
that survive, though you've cut briar,
shoveled roots when they've taken over.
A veteran of an old war once told me:
You'll never know how close we came
to losing the whole shebang.
And though I may listen
at the portal of his story, there'll be
no return to that time before the cloud,
before the world could destroy itself.
I like to think it's innocence I see
in his eye, also a vine, endless runners,
a young man reaching
through brambles for a berry.

A Late Summer Memory

I used to lay in the grass
and watch a grasshopper's jaw wobble
in horizontal grind,
which seems an odd way to nibble
your food. *He'll spit tobacco juice on you,*
my great-grandma would say
from the loft of her eighth decade
when one lit on my arm.

They still come flying at bare legs
late August, striking like soft straw
until the chill lames their voices.
Leaving me to stand in the dew
with singing creatures who have so few
hours in this world, and wonder
what the old woman meant.

Small

A balsam fir, no more than
six inches high,
makes its bonsai thrust
between rows of rock trenched

for flowers, plants its moon stake
between hours of labor.
One shift of stone could end
the selfish root, leaving aura,

echo: *I would have this spot.*
As though we choose our place
to enter the world (why here?) then push up
from earth, willing to be crushed.

My childhood eyes find small things,
peer out from the split
seed, flea beetle, nub of pinecone.
From such vision, branches grow.

Box Fan

You can find one in a junk store
fifty years old, still oscillating,
gristled cord that begs
the question of *what lasts?*
Yearly, my dad wedges our fan
in a window, blowing outward
at night, to pale trysts of moths,
swearing it pulls air inside.
Its voice of cool dust
softens edges of knives and tables,
sharp things that cannot hurt us,
padded in gauzes of breeze.
And so much humming! Cicada

scales, oiled blades, my mother's
absent drone as we put away work,
undressing the day. Our house sleeps hard,
breathes like a child pressed by
August heat. If there is allegory
in the wheel's spin—If, in fact
its small motor turns the stars
or some larger axis,
none of us is the wiser, caught up
in shucking corn, snaps of beans
for canning, left to dry on towels
at night, in the wind my father
turns inside out.

Pneumonia weather,

some call it, as gulf heat floats
by cloud, milk-coats the mountains
where we like to say

fool's spring, when lady slippers
swarm wetland shores in furrows.
At the bottom of the creek,

minnows wake, my dad skinnies
down the bank like a boy,
wades shallows below a cabin

he will not finish building. Before
the last nail, peach blossoms
fall on snow, frogs fold back to mud.

Old man's friend, they call this
sickness of warm and cold, its lungs
a dry rattle of leaves among

a stand of mourners. *Oh, gusts
of wind*, how you make ice
melt out of time, send ripples

across this cupped bowl of hands
I dip and raise in borrowed
portions I can never return.

Coloring Leaves in Grade School

Children rise in frost to gather
leaves before school,
the upright methodist oak,
sugar maples in nimble dances,

soft gold pools of poplar
fans, hung in banners before
tracing paper. By our own
push, the crayon's rub

scans each vein and form,
opens the palm of geographies;
forks, curves, and reversals
in light wanderlust on the page.

It seems magic,
this flurry of small hands,
and who but a child could bear
such irradiations of shape,

lost lines and torn edges--
the whole sum of our stories
emerging one morning,
that quickly, that suddenly.

My Grandfather Dug Coal

To be your granddaughter is to know
earth's darkness,
different than night,

the kind where you dream
seams of garnet left by stars.

Not just a combustible hunk
of cold, not just one way out,
and a ceiling of shale

ready to choke-damp the tunnel
between you and your seven kids.

Because of you, the sky opens
into lapis, sun showers the gliding chair

where I sit and watch beetles
clamber from small shafts,
the voles soft ramble toward

an exit I can never seem to find.

To be your granddaughter,
is to know the mountain that's been
torn, plowed, blasted.

You didn't know you'd die at thirty-three,
you just kept

swinging that big lamp
toward the outbye at quitting time,
burrowing up towards light.

Moonset

You swim the tops of trees,
the lowest you can go
without touching skin.
Sleepless, I used to trifle you
with questions like who I'd marry,
would I have a daughter.
You listened, pulling tides
over sand. Now, light leaves
its sea for a mountain,

a field. Beyond pink tufts
of mimosa, shines the hard
dust of all the lives
ever offered, the ones
not chosen, weightless,
cold and planetary. The first
cardinal of the morning
shadows a branch, a dark face
the moon unmasks.

Family Cabin in a Coal Town

Backed up to brambles, tar paper
turns slick crimson from rain,
ores of iron. Ghosts of tenant labor
climb roof to sky, where

a small, dark head of chimney
pokes up, watching the road--
which was not a road when it was built,
but dirt trail or horse path.

I don't know its history,
the mountain cuts off light by noon,
and that is that, rooms doused,
windows never lit, porches never

whining under cane rockers.
That's how quickly a home becomes
a shroud, vines of dusty flowers
climbing a cold stove. I brush

off the grate, the bent pipe,
look for what's lost, believing
like the bright, blue morning glories
who can find most anything.

Where I Started Long Ago

It's been a long spell since
I've watched trees shadow the grass,
how daily they make and unmake

time, shrink in noon sun,
stretch toward evening to grab
at the fence festooned

in orange trumpet. And what
lengthens here if not the girl
with a stick and calluses, who climbs

she thinks, toward light?
Shade pigments the yard, imprint
of summer, an umbra you lean into,

darker version of yourself.
An ear to the ground brings
deep green singing, what memory is

to a child, full of whistles and wings
rubbed against one another.
We share a shifting edge,

those leaved images and me,
a drifting I can never appease,
an end that never really matters.

Memory Fragment at Dawn

The yard is a mess of small shadows
playing inside the larger
shadow that is night's half-turn.
A groundhog humps along

the fence, makes his blurred
way home. For no reason,
the umbra that is my mother
takes shape, sponges again the sand

from my eyes, lifts me to a stream
I can't see. The song of the water
is cool, like the white-throated
sparrow in still-dark trees,

or perhaps it's only a brown thrasher,
calling and calling away
some loose grit of sleep
with her hard, mineral light.

One Morning During Advent

My neighbor's horse takes his first
steps from a darkened barn,
sashays towards a field
whose light seems tentative,

like it might be snatched away.
There is no record of what
moved in the night, or yesterday—
just a long space between fences,

and a turning towards me,
of that mane waving like grain.
It isn't even the sun's rise,
but his soft thud on silence,

that spurs the swept pasture,
a shoulder's ripple and reddening
until the sky itself breaks tether.
Just like that, a warm body

can change a whole landscape—
racing toward the apple
packed in my pocket, as if
it's the only bright star.

Evening Creek

A creek toward nightfall does not sing,
but testifies in bits and pieces
of what grows along its banks,
fern and fronds playing the waves,
ripped and ransomed
and bound for mouths of oceans.
It's not for love of water or moon
that we pause to listen, but flood--
that picks up the stray riders
in our veins and never has a name.
In my life, I have not loved
in quite the way I wanted, sigh drooping
willows, but that is only the stream's
mischief, the way crawdads change
their minds, swim backwards.

Hollyhocks are springing up

against fencerows, tin-roofed barns
outdoor privies—any place they can
lean like tired ladies in bright bonnets.
Shithouse flowers, local boys call them,
as if we need another reason
for the head to mock the heart.

They are the pink of leftover valentines,
what you'd buy in the five-and-dime
for two bucks a box, the color
of peppermint after you've chewed it.
I think the blossoms prefer common names,
(bellflower, forget-me-not, bleeding heart)

to Latin. Things spring up around a name,
people hang on to names after
divorce and death. *Homo sapiens*, we're called,
and I worry about where wisdom
will come from, what the flowers will rest
against when the old walls are gone.

October on Eleanor Street

Harry called,
the note says ringed in lamplight.

And I want to call you back,
send you skating and falling
in the street, where a harvest
moon casts its brass glow
over asphalt's scrawled chalk
obscenities, over oil slick rainbows
of a garage now closed,
in a closed corner of the city.
Where board and nail
keep out what's forgotten

anyway, all of it touched by
night-blooming moonflower.
Look up, I want to say,
before we forget to notice
how light hangs tinsel
on unhitched boxcars, unhinges
doors, shatters windows;
how it chances everything.

Beech Tree

A spread of high roots
runs naked so you can see those thick
peasant feet working the dirt

like men plowing shoeless.
A knobby cast of ants and lizards,
the occasional leaf

wafts cerebral, its gray trunk
filled with eyes of ancestors. I won't call
it wiser, but worn in the way

of a boot, dirty and storied
with something to say. Even in sleep
the tree marks itself,

carves a braille of history
on flesh pocked by burl or gall.
I don't know if it's beautiful

or deep down ugly-- only that
I too have scars and have grown
somehow around them.

Fall Equinox

Sounds of steady falling—
ping of green acorns on dirt,
and late peaches hard-balling
the shed roof.

Not a heavy package of grief,
not that sack of mail on the porch,
but a crow's omen of leavings,
evenings when the sky

shines its beet red edge below
the moon's harp and horn.
Where summer plays out, backflows,
has itself a spell, knots

the strings between halves until
they quiver, stretched and singing
between split paths.

On the Lawn of the Hotel Chamberlain

There are three kinds of twilight,
measured by degrees
above or below the horizon.
I think one is called nautical,
but we do not gauge hours
this way. It's like are the stars visible
yet, can we hide the hand
you slip under my top as we walk.
It's all slosh and bones of sea
creatures by the bay, lobster-
red streaks of eventide break
waves, painting noses of dolphin,
the hair on your arm pink. Somehow,
the aged stone wall holds back
water, refuses to let the sun sink.
But that is another kind of twilight,
whose dark/bright
days go unmeasured, whose warm
salt glaze freezes the skin forever.

A day moon

persists the length of November,
floats on hickory smoke,
tracks like a hound.

They say her presence
means a soul flown earth
watches us above sugar maples,

orb, then half-orb
that howls to the eye,
makes it look behind at what hovers.

Gray shadows moth-print
her face, scowls of an old
midwife stirring tonic

in the dust, still as the pause
between gusts of wind.
Or maybe after all,

it's the moon hare (They say rabbits like cold),
that freezes over our shoulders,
frayed light in tandem

with all distant, crumbling bodies,
these mere clots of fur
that tether us to time.

A Sudden Splash in the Pond

A bass leaps the water,
hatched from eggs that lay
in mud for who knows how long,
now startling the dove-gray
waves that push reflections
of branches right up to shore.
I've no particular business
with pond life, but wonder
at how things abide, or glide listening,
how even in deep spaces of bodies,
cells of stars gel and coalesce
to sleek, sudden presence.
I wish I had a parable for fish
short of scripture, how at a given
moment, holiness surfaces
in the splash of unexpected
sparkle cutting the murk,
grabbing cold-blooded at the sun.

A Shovel in the Rain

A derelict shovel leans
against the side of the house, propped
since planting season.

It can spend weeks this way,
set apart like tools on a pegboard,
caked, with nothing to beat

off the dirt where its old shine
hides, no human hand to dig
until some green and distant

memory gleams back. Nothing to make
you think of it there,
until one night in bed, rain comes,

the first hard plops
playing flat notes on steel. Then treble,
up and down the scale, collar ringing,

choruses on the tip, kickplate pinging up
into some high range of longing
you can't even sing.

Perry County, 1968

It's learning the way
around horse trails, civil war
paths in hardwood blaze,
gray ghosts the eye comprehends,
then doesn't, a child
lugging only a slingshot.
All the lives that ever languished—
eulogized by the north fork,
cadence in silver rings
tumbling over shale,
echoing the escarpment in strings,
finely woven, translatable
if you follow them, as soldier,
map-maker of a wilderness.
To maneuver the mountain
in summer is to memorize oil lamps
swinging in the dark, hooves
stamping against the heart,
bearing up loneliness embittered
as hickory smoke, this world
that does not wake from its dream

Something More

There's more to it, farmers say,
more than one kind
of brilliance,
the nimbus luring prey animals
from dens, plants that open
toward evening—

foamflower, night lily, moonflower.
You can plant by country dark,
ask the secret questions of your life;
how perennials come back,
how the moon's unspooling
siphons water up to moisten

seeds. A fence halts the eye--
It's always been that way,
a rail you'd gladly cross over
returning as a new, tender leaf,
raised by the shining constants
of *was* and *is* and *will be.*

Kitchen Table

It's all yellow formica and elbows,
a permanent crust of gravy
at one end and cigarette burns,
benedictions of wind like
cold butter blowing outside.
It's where the first ripe peaches

sweeten my tongue, where lists
for the IGA get written in cursive
curls and cues. My mama can't
cook for dirt but likes recipes
which she calls out to me,
in layers of warm spice cake,

as I memorize the curve of her arm
while she beats the batter.
Try as I might, I can't find the heart
of this family, it's somewhere
in the tabletop, grinds and sighs
we draw from inside its stained contours,

our work made of quiet forms
known to us, knives and spoons
that live together. It's where we leave
a cut in the shining top, where
an onion sliced in half shows us
the myriad routes to its center.

Field Notes on Time

Is brother a man now? I ask
as a child, noting he's grown tall.
Why would you ask a thing
like that, my mama says when
she won't answer.

I get it now, the blurred
linear of age, where the story
of time, if time exists,
hides in tenses of river rock,

past, present, future—
stones blown in from deep
space. There's no choice
but to scoop dirt in your palm,
keep burrowing on inside
the mystery.

Know the mossy banks are this:
span, stretch, stint, cycle.
Water filling water as we wrinkle.

Some tribes see time
as a big circle,
clouds that rain and rise
white again, rot that springs
up wild alder and sedge.

I'd like to ask
my mama, how many blue moons
have risen over the creek
since my birth, and hear
the stream inside her splash back:
Thirteen.

The mourning dove

sends her perfect dirge
woodwind along the jeep trail
at noon. Veiled, her flute
might be Choctaw or Seminole
divining a trail of tears
through air and pine,
ghostly gifts left to us. In early

memory, my great-grandmother
rocks me, her tobacco wad
in cheek, speaking of bitter
Kentucky winters, dark-jawed coal
mines, whiskey that turns
a man mean right where he's born,
then outlasts him. I gaze delighted

and fat, the way hills keep
thrusting up in bloom
and sycamores unhewn, swell
mirrored in elder eyes. Reflecting
as infants do, the gray light
of creatures born into this world
to utter its shrouded sadness

Hunter's Moon

Walking home at dusk
skies dilate, the headlight spelling
after me is the moon,
sanguine elder of roads,
fields, and slanted barns.

Deer come out to feed
on fallen grains, rye or timothy
laid out cold in lunar
eye, pelts blurring beside
the blood moon,

as though fading in place.
Days woven in leaves
unlace themselves, light
of another kind scales fences,
enters to wreck the temple.

Habits of Being

The doll I recall
has bright blue eyes and wets
when you give it water,
not soft to hold but I like
making it do things.
My mother says *peel me*
some potatoes and I learn
not to carve away too much white.
Or *clean me some beans*,
and I separate the tiny gray rocks
from pintos, cull the stray
shrivels from our pot,
grit that is our lot and lesson.
Who are we, but two bodies
in twilight, whose habits move
forward in muscle memory--
Into a future where my hands
by small acts, form her again,
filling the kitchen, all absence
born by the dishrag hung
back on its hook, resuming its place.

Just Before Hard Winter

Leaves hang in copper coils,
cardinals pick up speed
flashing redder days. We're always
reminding each other
how quickly it gets dark,
as if life is now a circle of sun
to be chased around,

faces tilted to the last ray
before extinction. A few miles
over our heads, air ceases
to hold the tiniest lung,
turns blood pure blue, the heart's
frozen lake. Any winged
unrest, we replace with fire,

licking up toward eternities
of dead stars-- this warmth
between us, all that we have.

II

So teach us to count our days, that we may gain a wise heart.

—Psalm 90:12

Tally

My hand raises by rote
to brush away a seed-sized
bug jostling along the spine
of a book. And he is fragile,
fragile as paper floating
the poles of the earth
in thin airplanes. Such is our habitus,
my too strong swat. We're
oversized in our gardens,
too heavy a burden
for crepe urgencies of spring.

I wonder what the final tally
of life will be, how many
beetles squashed underfoot,
how many moths carelessly
admitted to the light of their death.
Or will the sad-eyed dog
I took in, held to my chest
for fourteen years, fold us at last
to our truer shapes, origami
of the pale beige wings
we wished always to be.

The Cove at Season's End

Late fall opens the cove
that teemed over a warm season
beyond reach, briar crosses
and copperheads ready to raise
their seals, now vanished.
Where life was, then wasn't,
the empty house
of childhood, her shoe's flat
echo stifled in stands
of beautyberry. All summer
the young chirped then rose,
old verses of toads ringing
call and response in mosses,
fossils of songs written
and left. I know that to enter here,
is to become the fox
an elliptical shape skirting a tree
line, hungering after bones.
Only vines of bittersweet
glory up a pole, pay no mind
to leavings, waving at geese
who fly in vees, straight
for the sycamore, then curve
as if deciding by afterthought,
they are done here.

The Broom

It used to be I'd notice the round
season of roses, May to October,
browning at the edges.
But then it became Sunday mornings,
coffee turned cold too soon, filter dry
as a cicada hull, the day beating
faster against my chest.
It's the tempo of slow constants
that changes, where hours spent
hugging the flaws of the body
won't pass at all. Or the child's nap,
that elastic hour of wide-eyed
stretch where I listen, keeping time
with my grandmother's corn broom
hushing the floor. Believing in its
spell of dust to halt the clock,
as she raises a cloud over my sleep,
squints into late afternoon sun and knows better.

The Norfolk Southern

There's a spot down the gravel road,
where the train curves close
enough to read painted logos, hear
its language I've forgotten

made of whippoorwills, the moon's bright
stamp on a cloud. A random stand
of bloodwort watches too, tangled
at my ankles, dusted by the hot iron

chug where I see my sister and me,
eternally kids, grifting beside the tracks
for rocks. Granite or quartz prizes
in piles of gravel, maybe we play

a little *chicken* then, make the horn
blow its horsepower and diesel
our way. It's good to have a place
so much yours you can die

there if you choose, pockets loaded
with secret stones. A man pauses
between boxes to wave, ponytail,
red kerchief in the wind,

where stacked platforms fly by
into a distance whose destination
I could look up-- But maybe this once
I can let it go, not know the end.

Sweeping the Porch

It all ends up here, pollen and petals,
then brown leaves in layers

on ailing boards that creak
since their nailing fifty years ago,

back when people
sat among each other, thickening

like lilies of an evening. I still keep
a broom handy, sweep four seasons

of wind-lost orphans—beech nut or acorn,
magnolia blossoms at the door's

surprised threshold, untried and virgin.
At this age I can't help but notice

what I looked past as a girl,
how a snail freezes on the flowerpot,

dead, then inches away,
or a piece of blue eggshell turns up,

brightening the steps. At such times, light
flings itself to the chore's

back and forth rhythms, rough-edging
bristles that snag the door key

secreting its shine under the grit
of the mat and sweeps it away.

A Rare Penny

They'll quit making them soon,
the boys who placed them
on the tracks in hot sun

will also disappear,
along with striped candy, cased
in jars on store counters. Gone, the hand

digging linty pockets for copper,
gone Lincoln's side gaze
in one-cent sized bubble

gum slots. And though no one
remembers, the first minted coin
bore a woman's head

of wild, flowing hair. She vanished
like the passenger pigeon,
the dodo and golden toad.

Like our pennies now spilled
in the dirt, not worth picking up,
though one day we'll go

walking to look for just one left
in the glass and weeds, along road
after road after road.

After Rain

It's the unstoppable shear
after rain, rivulets on windows,

ditches rising to reveal a child's
red ball, half a pair of pliers,

strands of a feed sack—all downstream,
the rivering of the forgotten.

How after the drumming fist
pushes things out of order, you wake

to a jumble of pasture, wild with parts
and pieces. Where light the color

of new corn, arches over a fence,
the doe picks her way in after-drizzle,

reassembles the field's fragments
by her presence. Clearing limbs

away in late afternoon, you ask
about this place you've come to;

what it is, whether it can be fixed,
whether you might recognize it again.

In Search of the Mythical Eagle

My neighbor says he saw
thirty eagles at once
in Virginia, by a salmon pond
near the place three rivers
trade fortunes, the harbor's waves
sloshing in bored renewal.
They've grown wise I suppose,
to the stocked waters,
shopping for fish from currents
high over the yule sparkle
of December. The marshes may
stay unfrozen for weeks,
all through the holy days
to hard winter. It's beautiful
and kind of sad when you think
of how they light down
and fill up at this table in times
of collapse as close by, people step
from stores in the snow,
flushed and shivering
like tall birds on a shore.

For Love of a Small Life

My grandma sets out to walk
stoop-shouldered up the slope
to her garden, the soft mounds
of her back like hills where you plant
vines of squash and melon.
She might well be dragging a plow
whose tines break up hard
luck soil, sending you home
with a mess of greens, greener
than a dollar. It's all in the hand's
remand, this small life,
cupped like a pea in the palm.

It's barely light when she climbs
from her high bed,
rolls out biscuits, then ascends
in vapors floating the mountain.
Every time I watch her walk off
I learn a little more about who I am.
On the morning she doesn't
come back, I will stay here
on the lowest knoll, kneel
where shelly beans spread
wings in dew and keep on picking.

Lady of Shalott

The dressing table doesn't hold much—
Evening in Paris, a comb,
camel-colored pumps tucked
below chestnut drawers.
My mother poses
wide-mirrored in sepia lens,
scarlet blush, tight sweater.
And like women of her era,
brooding brow, hand cocked
on hip, a dark star captured
by arched glass. Behind
and on each side, walls
and more walls to wrap around
the small blond girl building
shadows with her hands.

Kitchen Epiphany

The cabinets are painted white
over old pine, shelves that slip
at one corner, causing jelly jars
to skate toward the counter
in rainbow skirts. Still sturdy
enough to hold a five-pound sack
of flour for years, or cornmeal

gone to mealy bugs. *Do you mind*
them, my grandmother asked me
once, and I didn't. Not much bother
enters the lemony light, its window
over the sink where a sprayer
works sometimes, or not. Always a rag,
pots taking a breather to soak,

time to pause and look
out where the propane tank sits,
a nest under its lid. For the longest
time, I'd watch that bird fly
in and out, spring riding its wings
like the shine of a spoon. Not knowing
it was a Carolina Wren, until one day, I did

Wine Goblets, Williamsburg 1986

They promised a sturdiness
back then, thrown
by wheel, packed in plain newsprint.

The girl I was,
lifts heavy, hardened clay to her chest,
a bearer of weight. She was,

is, a mystery of summer blankets,
long, Socratic parleys
into boys, reds and whites

spilling love's slights and scrapes.
Each goblet is a perfect
hollow where a river runs,

even in my dark cabinet
of spoiled light. Even here,
the moon's fat face cries *fill me.*

Wild Onions

For Isabella

My 6th great grandmother
rests in Virginia dirt, wild onions
on her grave. She lived a good

life, so declare the stringy tops
who archive deeds of the dead.

Daffodils grow close by, but what
can a flower ever know
of things a woman will do to survive?

Ubiquitous as rain, the bitter
greens; onion, mustard, dandelion,

offer a slim bite at winter's end,
fill apron whisperings of wool
on mud. A maid's harvest of mostly

skin and translucency, ghostly
snap of a radish. Trees, still leafless,

stoop at river's edge like the back
of a gathering woman, rooted
in her measure of shadows,

stains of grassy light on the tips
of her fingers.

Distances

An acre away, staccato
of a screech owl, plucking
strings of blackness
to a stiff quiver. Also a mouse
hiding from anything gold
and round; eyes of birds,

the moon when it's low.
Along pastures, bittersweet vine,
not ripe yet, clenches its fist
around posts, tightening
its hold as night skids
to free fall. Far and overhead,

two astronauts stuck in orbit,
watch sparklers of war spread
middle and east, wait for winter
when they can come home,
bathed in ice and waves.
As though to call them

back to us, a nearby neighbor
turns on his floodlight,
beams through woods and nests
at shattering speeds,
until it touches the outer ring
of the long, dark field.

Lightning Bugs

At summer's first flash
we scare up a mason jar
from its dirt cellar, punch air holes
with a butcher knife. We swipe
at blackness and snap lids,
snaring an immeasurable cosmos
that blinks steady comfort
on night tables, off and on
like my uncle's turn signal
before it gave out. The glass
burns to gray ash while we sleep,
missing the dim throb
of final light. Last times are like that,
a loved one waits for the room
to empty, then dies. And though
we intend to set the bugs loose,
we forget, slipping out of sight
ourselves, as the sky beyond
keeps coming in dark waves.

Crooked Trees

Trees on the river bank
have never been tended,
branches set out in one direction

then whipsaw back, like a two-headed
snake. Undressed in winter,
a naked desire for light

is all they've known, canopied
by the limbs of others.
For every bit of sky, a grapevine

to lasso the love of sun,
bring it down in a crack.
They've struggled, these trees,

such as to break a heart,
but so much of life is unwitnessed,
a face blurred in the water,

swimming alone. They say a crooked
twig is bent by dead spirits
pointing direction. But what

have you ever told me, ancestors,
but to turn toward the stream,
follow it home like a horse.

Greasy Spoon 5:00 a.m.

A street's dead end, a dive no one
knows but the working guys,
tires to their hips, tight black T-shirts
like crows, flitting in and out

of trucks. Opening just as night
goes starless, a lit gold window
the only marquis for shadows
creeping the alley shortcut

to a grilled honey bun. No talk,
just *what'll it be*, these shop class
boys grown older, and me with
eyes still deciding between

light and dark. Then the soft, sweet
thing that tastes of nascent
figures in moonlight,
the cinnamon-dusted return

below tremors of leaves pasted
to the dawn, and feathered shapes
of men in treetops, calling
down arias all the way home.

Visions

> "Now during all this time, from beginning to end, I had two kinds of understanding" —Julian of Norwich

A room, a world,
small hazelnut glazing the palm.
When asked of its size,
she replies: *It is all that is made,*
meaning the whole of space,
every orbit that shines
round or oval like a shell.
What lasts and ever shall,
what the astronaut sees,
no intercessor to explain,
nor saint, as from thousands
of miles he understands
finally, what tiny is—
a lost blue earring he can blot
out by raising a thumb.
Gone then, history and zebras,
DaVinci and peas—And all of us
strangely happy to let the darkness
consume us in peace

Inheriting My Father's Watch

It's stopped at two minutes after twelve,
the portal you exit through
carried home in my mother's lap.

Not to make it grander than it is,
feign craftsmanship, or declare the elegant
sweep of a minute-hand,

yours being an engine of quartz
and electrical charges, stainless steel band
of a man who comes home each night.

You tell me to eye its ticking during flights
to settle a dizzy stomach,
that the rotor winds a mainspring,

depends on the swing of arm and wrist.
I want to wake it up,
that movement, to find in the rewinding,

questions time itself might ask such as
when were you happiest?
Or twisting off case and crystal,

unseal a bezel to listen for the lifting
of you, beyond its calibre
clock-beat, to cloud, then blue.

Water Speaks and is Gone

In a country of streams, old tires
lodge rim deep. They've known
rain and the yellow call of rain's
coming. I tell people
I'm a child of the hollows,
my claim to the rain crow,
my mother's memory of flood
waters rutting down the mountain
where I was conceived. At night,
creeks still stumble toward home,
hill-heavy ghosts of my people
rowing in moon's sheen, bodies
made new and perfect. Their green
waves flow but also stay, water
that weighs in true, or doesn't.
Call a name and its timbre comes
back to you, caught up against
a slab of sheet metal shored
in a bend. Or plays a banked washboard,
tin-strung echo of a song you think
you know, but might be your own voice
beating on the back of a river.

The World Reveals Itself

When I walk, I don't look
for anything but what sees fit
to find me, even if *holy*
is just a load of railroad

ties soaked in creosote that smells
up the tracks nearby. Or oak giants
who splay fingers, owning
the grab of pasture, blue-gray

shade painting the grass,
penumbra blown by wind so you
can play that child's game
of trying to stay in the light

as it leaps away.
A shifting hopscotch of chance,
where you notice your thoughts,
for the first time in years,

do not trouble you. Some long, languid
muscle stretches its summer arms
and legs, speaks the hard,
the soft, in breezy steps

patterned by trees. A simple clod
of dirt rolled between fingers
feels cool, made of black flies,
and shadows, then mostly sun.

Fall's Labor, Fall's Memory

Suppose this day's rake and heave
is a room I'll forget in ten years,
but for an image or two—Will it be
red-orange leaves cindering

the stoop, boots wet with dew
drying on the sidewalk, leaking
small shadows at their heels?
Light knits together twig

and inchworm, brushes my hand
as it sweats. I pry up rocks from clay,
and hope I'll recall the heat
between arm and shovel, a goodness

of work sparking between steel
and flint. This time of year, people
burn in barrels, smoke the air
with old things they've let go.

But we never really know
what we'll long for later, whose face
might flutter down a scaffold
of color. There are questions

I'd ask my dad if he were still alive.
He'd pause with his rake and say,
well, let me think now……
Then would, as best he could, remember.

Crepe Myrtle

They say if you walk beneath one,
the perfect direction of life unfolds,

a petaled shore, the cane's slow
thickening to light our days

of trial and error. Or so the proverb
reigns over summer's end,

running smooth-armed, peeling bark
where flesh meets air, soft stare

of spindles that seem to point
everywhere and all at once. None of us gets

to foretell her own course,
but *oh, limbs of autumn, can you see it now—*

the child that once was,

a finger raised to her grandma's wallpaper
tracing a pink vine of blooms

room to room, to its final, burst of flowers.

The Well

Past the second field in misted hickory,
lurks an old cistern used for cattle in its day,

curtained by moss. Make no mistake,
things get covered over in time,

rising eventually, every vine a patina
of green memory. My grandma had a well

where we'd lean and echo down
fieldstone, or draw on bucket and pulley

once lowering a barn cat,
the light scratch of shame as it shot

back out. I recreate a story, missing light
and shadows, which is the mystery of remembrance,

the mind's wiring to a world more fluid
than we can perceive. In a picture,

my grandma stands by her well, old gray dress
the color of rock facing, eleven children

raised to full height—evidence there's
a grace in the design of living, patterns

by which things live and die. As kids,
we pretend, inchoate souls filling in blanks

we'll amend later, seeing through a watery
lens, what ought to have killed us and didn't.

A Haunting at Willard Creek

It's a fearsome yarn, a smokehouse
haunted by love turned bitter
as hung pig flesh. Our mother
won't walk past it at dusk

when the sky drapes blackbird
wings over the dirt road.
We ask often for the tale,
our desire for it, a coal's ember

that blinks back on no matter
how often you douse it. It's always
the same; a man's eye, a woman
caught skipping under the stars

with no father or brother--
What had to be cut,
and cut down. Sometimes the details
change and we say – *No, it was*

this way, and I wonder at how
childhood is both weightless
and concrete, the moon's black blood
a thing we have to get straight

like any item of inheritance.
When my mama has gone around
the mountain, the story will be mine
to tell and tell differently.

Stories

> oh, children, think about the good times
> —Lucille Clifton

It's odd to think of a mother
longing for something,
especially when you're a child,
round and egocentric as the moon.

But I know mine did, her face
lit by whiskey's constant itch,
which never mattered really—
Who questions the light

on its source? Late, when stars peek
through a loose curtain,
the gauzy film around her
floats in night wind, stories

hidden in the pleats of her nightgown
sail around the room--
Of how she flew on grapevine
when no older than me,

face tilted to the sky, its calliope
swing like the dances of dead
uncles and cousins who open
our kitchen door and take

a turn on the linoleum's grit.
Tiny moths and fireflies gather
to hear what I hear, slipping
torn screens, bodies in waltz

that lie pasted on the mesh,
come morning, wings flaccid,
spread out, not so much like a smile
but the memory of one.

Afton Mountain

You never know what the weather
will be doing on the mountain,
people say, and you know

they're from here, where wind
grips and pulls your shirt
as it chooses, dressing over

what is perfect and stiff.
It's been known to graft
an apple or tell a valley

the pleasures of low places
how spring begins in shadows, then climbs
its way up. I think it was May

when our hands found each other
like a couple of sad, old hounds,
and we bore diamond kites to the top,

hero-themed, watching as Batman, Wonder
Woman, emperors, and moth-winged
mermaids, all released at once.

Ball Lightning

It rolls across my grandma's
kitchen floor, the day her boy
dies in the African campaign,
second war, a hot August
when gardens lie festered.
She knows then by sign,
the cloud that falls to earth,
blue-white ball of news
in its teeth. It's the way of fire,
to brag on what it burns
before a man can knock at the door,
tell you what electricity
already told you on the quiet
linoleum. There are stories
that need telling twice,
before it sinks in, flame first, then flesh,
a hammer in the sky,
a chair pushed from the table.

Voices From Coal Country

Rock of Ages, cleft for me
let me hide myself in Thee
--A.M. Toplady

I.
My grandmother hums and watches
the cliff near her porch, green in moss
overlay, same as every day
of summer. What we call *our own*
people live strewn, seeded from
the cabin that fades on fieldstone
one hill over, owl-owned among poplar,
opposite where the sun rises.

II.
Falling rock zone.
My father explains as we drive hairpins,
now and then a boulder pocked
dead gray as the moon, watches
us pass. There are eyes
everywhere, in the new
pine trees, wobbly as colts.
Someone planted them on flat
places that were once peaks.

III.
They got their coal and got out.
We boil water when the news
says we should, though the creek
beats itself clean like clothes.
My kin in cane rockers, begin
their sway, they say *it's easier to hear
a thing that's moving.*
For a time, we listen to each
other's limbs creaking in the dark.

IV.
*My skin is sweet milk,
pouring from the limestone cleft
into my granddaughters'
mouths, open and laughing.
A hawk's nest hides
in the crevices, I watch them fly
to and fro, pale blue eggs
the color of my first church
dress. This is how I see
us; keening in wide circles
for the cracked shells.*

V.
Children of the hollows,
we play on the great rock
come dusk, toeholds in ridges
carved a million years ago.
My grandmother inhales
all the shadows, leaving us light.
We've come with colored pencils,
to draw ourselves in pastel
on the level, petroglyphs
that claim we are *here*. None of us
knows how long a name will last

September

Hurricanes move up the coast,
inland in waves of salted clouds,
breezes strum gray washboard
tunes on sentries of summer's end.
But softer, this sea wind,
you listen to it pull fine
twine through muted forms and figures,
giving them voice. Walnuts whistle
as they roll, the cast-off cinder block
hums in baritone from weeds,
Wingstem sheds its singing fringe,
adding to layers of leaves, rendering
the path home, obscured.
That's when you stand castaway,
hearing first, the raven's ruffled crown,
then the ridges and grooves
of crickets, the light hiss of fences,
played and giving way, then finally
the larger song beneath it all.

Metamorphosis

Summer turns mean past a point,
sends poison you don't need,
like caterpillars fat as green cigars
spiked up to sting. Enveloped
is a moth, wings soft as spring
grass, who will one day unseal
the glue binding her to dirt.
What I've never understood
is the nature of custody on earth,
the casings that hold us,
whether it's true as they say,
the scant three feet between
this world and the other.
When August coughs up dust
it's easy to see only its clouded
carapace. You forget how
even a blank-eyed worm
can punch out a miracle,
rise stunningly alive to air.

How Old Life Breaks Loose

There's a moth on the screen,
rusted dry in cold,

russet with black-tipped wings.
I wonder why this cold mesh,
whether she was headed

to a warm chink in the siding
or attic vent. Or believed
she'd slip the sash and sleep,
suspended for winter, between life

and death, borderland
where fluttering is a long dream.

I know that place, or think I do—
Where we intend to stop,
then go on. Then held by a thin hair,

upside down, heart-shaped,
not even a rattle as wind,

in the end, pries our ashes from a wire.
Torn away, as if this spot
has held for us, nothing but light.

Rain Song

Rain is the oldest grandmother
after rock, clear enough
to soothe a child's fears
in the dark. You can hear
its arms swell up rivers,
slide down mountains of mud,
you can see, even at night,
that gray woman in hard shoes
from the dry goods store,
lace and unlace thunderheads
over all the fields.

Fifty years ago I learned to drive
in cloudbursts drowning
the windshield, wipers beating until they gave out.
Sometimes, I still have to pull over,
sit by a flooded ditch,
small and defeated, until droplets
thin to mist, the sky paints
its bow over cumulus towers.
Each leaf-tap a crone's ballad
of woe, that love, all its comforts,
are partial, the rain limitless.

The Story I've Come To

They beg notice above hardwoods,
vultures with hooked beaks
like can openers ready to rip.
I wonder what they've found—
Often, it's a beaver by the stream,

hounded to the bottom
of his slide path and killed
by people, as people do.
You walk into many deaths
when you enter the woods,
or maybe it's only language
that dies, the space it took
filled by wind and wood thrush.

But it's also here that life,
in fact, has no end at all.
Fallen trees, gray as old calluses,
host a flux of bright violet—
living that can't let the dead be.
I praise aloneness,
that the most gnawing losses
do not finish time that began

in a word—And encompass every
moment after, even my kick-scuff
gait, sound that shuffles
toward nothing and is happy there.
I won't claim any peace
with temporality, but what I've lost
has mostly been returned to forms
I can love again,

old faces shaded in ferns,
below lily-of-the-valley,
known to peek from columbine
where it grows wild.
And if I squint way out toward
the lower creek, I can see a girl who looks
like me, making her way over leaves,
closing the distance between us

Acknowledgements

These poems have appeared in the following journals:

Cutleaf Journal: "Family Cabin in a Coal Town," "Box Fan," "Lightning Bugs, "September"

Broad River Review: "Perry County, 1968"

Kestrel: "Visions"

Blue Mountain Review: "Crepe Myrtle"

Salvation South: "Kitchen Epiphany," "Norfolk Southern," "A Dry Spell in July They Say is Climate Change"

Image Journal: "Fall Equinox"

Book of Jobs Anthology : "My Grandfather Dug Coal"

Women Speak Anthology Vol. 11, Women of Appalachia Project: "A Kind of Music", "Metamorphosis"

Crab Orchard Review: "Rain Song"

About the Author

Sharon Ackerman lives in central Virginia with roots in Perry County, Kentucky where her ancestors established themselves over hundreds of years. Her writing is informed by the natural setting of coal-mining Kentucky, as well as the stories and cadences she carries forward as a child of the Appalachian Migration.

Ackerman's poetry has appeared in the *Atlanta Review, Southern Humanities Review, Valparaiso Poetry Review, Blue Mountain Review, Kestrel, Roanoke Review, Cutleaf Journal, Appalachian Places, Salvation South, Broad River Review* and several others. Her second poetry collection *A Legacy of Birds* (Kelsay Books, 2025) is available through Amazon. She is poetry editor for *Streetlight Magazine.*

www.ingramcontent.com/pod-product-compliance
Lightning Source LLC
LaVergne TN
LVHW051018080826
845145LV00009B/2680

* 9 7 8 1 9 6 3 1 1 0 2 3 4 *